GROWING UP IN THE
FIFTIES

Rebecca Hunter

HODDER
Wayland

Produced for Hodder Wayland by
Discovery Books Ltd
Unit 3, 37 Watling Street, Leintwardine, Shropshire SY7 0LW, England

First published in 2001 by Hodder Wayland, an imprint of Hodder Children's Books

British Library Cataloguing in Publication Data

Hunter, Rebecca,
    Growing up in the fifties
    1. Children - Great Britain - Social life and customs -
Juvenile literature 2. Great Britain - Social conditions-
20th century - Juvenile literature 3. Great Britain - Social
life and customs - 1945 - - Juvenile literature
    I. Title
    941 ' . 0855 ' 0922

    ISBN 0 7502 3548 9

Printed and bound in Grafiasa, Porto, Portugal.

Designer: Ian Winton
Editor: Rebecca Hunter

Hodder Children's Books would like to thank the following for the loan of their material:

Aquarius Library: page 22 (top), 23 (bottom); **Discovery Picture Library**: page 9 (inset),
11 (top), 13 (inset), 14 (inset); **Hulton Getty**: Cover, page 6, 10 (top) R. Bertram Unne, 10
(bottom) Bert Hardy, 11 (bottom) Charles Hewitt, 12, 14, 22 (bottom), 25, 29 (top), 30 (both);
The London Transport Museum: page 17 (top); **The Robert Opie Picture Collection**:
page 9 (top), 16 (top), 18 (bottom), 21 (middle), 24 (top), 27, 28.

Hodder Children's Books
A division of Hodder Headline Limited
338 Euston Road
London NW1 3BH

CONTENTS

THE 1950S

The 1950s was a time of great change. The world was recovering from the effects of the Second World War. Living standards rose as people earned more money and had more to spend it on. Young people's lives were particularly affected as American goods, music and fashion reached the shores of Britain. In this book, four people who were young in the fifties, tell us what their lives were like during these changing times.

ALLAN MARTIN

Allan Martin was born in 1948 in Scotland. His father was a policeman and he grew up in the area of King's Park, Glasgow.

▶ Allan in 1958 aged 10.

NORMA ROE

Norma Roe was born in 1949 in Chatham in Kent. She spent her childhood in a small village nearby.

▶ Norma in 1957 aged 8.

DAVID SANDS

David Sands was born in 1946. The family lived in Scotland where his father ran a motor business.

▶ David in 1950 aged 4.

ELIZABETH PANTON

Elizabeth Panton was born in 1942 in Shrewsbury. She has one brother and one sister and her father was a solicitor. The family lived in Shropshire.

▶ Elizabeth in 1950 aged 9.

Houses

In the early fifties there was a chronic housing shortage. Few houses had been built in the forties and many had been destroyed in the war. The government planned to demolish all slum buildings and build new houses. Some of them were in 'new towns', towns that were purpose-built rather than those that grew up naturally. By 1961, twenty new towns, many including huge, new council estates, had been built.

Norma

I grew up in a village near Chatham in Kent. In 1952 we moved into a new bungalow that my dad had designed and had built. After living in a small, old town house with an outside toilet, it was lovely to move into the spacious bungalow with a huge garden. My aunt, uncle and cousins lived next door, so there were always plenty of children to play with.

Many of the new houses were built at the edge of towns where there was more space. In the crowded towns themselves high-rise blocks of flats were built. At first, residents thought these new modern buildings were wonderful, but they were not good places for children to live.

Allan

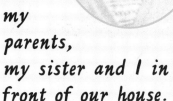

We lived in a ground floor cottage flat in Glasgow. It had been built in the 1940s in one of the new suburbs. This picture shows me and my mum outside it. I am wearing a kilt which I wore on Sundays and special occasions.

Elizabeth

My family lived in a large Victorian house in the small town of Market Drayton in Shropshire. This picture was taken by my brother and shows my parents, my sister and I in front of our house.

THEN & NOW

• In 1951, 30 per cent of people owned their own homes. By 1997, 70 per cent did.

At Home

Few married women went out to work in the fifties; most stayed at home and looked after their families.

David

My mum did not go out to work. She kept house for my dad, my brother, sister and myself as well as my grandad who lived with us.

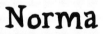

Norma

My dad was a civil servant and worked for the Ministry of Pensions. My mum did not go out to work but stayed at home looking after us. She was a clever dressmaker and made most of our clothes. She made me smocked dresses, and knitted jumpers and cardigans for us all. She also worked from home, making baby clothes to sell.

The quality of life improved for most housewives during the fifties. Housework became much easier as electric machines

became common in the new 'modern' houses.

"Here it is—the new electric cooker. Isn't it a beauty?"

Electric cookers, washing machines, and sewing machines all cut down the amount of time a housewife had to spend working.

Elizabeth

Although we lived in a big house, my mother did not have much help. A woman did come in to cook lunch on Sundays but we all had to help around the house. We also did a lot of work in the garden, weeding and chopping wood for the fires indoors. This picture shows me mowing the lawn.

SHOPPING

At the beginning of the fifties some foods were still in short supply and were still rationed. Rationing did not end completely until July 1954.

Most housewives shopped every day and visited many small shops: the butcher, greengrocer, baker and grocery store. The number of houses that had a refrigerator was still quite low, so keeping food fresh was a problem.

David

My mother went shopping every day. The grocer's sold sugar, tea and flour, which was measured out into thick, brown paper bags. Butter was chopped off a block and patted into shape with two wooden paddles. The butcher's shop had sawdust on the floor and animals hanging on rails above. Once a week the vegetable man came round the back lanes with a horse and cart, selling fresh fruit and vegetables.

Old Money

Before decimalization, British currency was made up of pounds, shillings and pence.

There were twelve pence (12d) in a shilling, and twenty shillings (20/-) in a pound. £5 notes were large and white.

Most of the food that people ate in the fifties was produced in Britain. What foods were in the shops depended on the season. Fresh fruit was often only available in the summer and autumn. Many people grew their own vegetables in their garden or allotment. At other times of the year, only tinned or bottled fruit and vegetables were available.

SELF SERVICE

During the fifties, shopping began to change dramatically with the introduction of the self-service supermarket. In 1956 more than six hundred self-service shops opened in the country. By the end of the fifties, most towns had a supermarket.

SCHOOL IN THE FIFTIES

After the war many couples started families, which resulted in what is called the 'post-war baby boom'. By the fifties these children were ready to go to school and so new schools were built. They were large, bright buildings which replaced the rather dark, cramped pre-war schools. The new schools had many more facilities than the old schools, with science labs, libraries and playing fields.

Norma

When I was 8, I moved to a new junior school. It had just been built to serve the new council estate that had grown up nearby. It was a lovely building with big, light rooms and had fields all around it where we played sport and went on nature trails. I was very happy at school. I was good at most subjects and played in several sports teams. This picture was taken at school.

Allan

My favourite lessons at primary school were drawing and painting. I hated writing with a pen and ink, as I was left-handed and so smudged everything. The teachers tried to force me to write with my right hand, but they never succeeded!

David

As well as reading, writing and arithmetic, we did lots of hand-work. We made lots of useless things out of cardboard and raffia! Punishment at school was usually being beaten with a strap and you could get it for almost anything: bad behaviour, being late, bad writing. Playtime was the best part of school. We usually played ball games until somebody smashed a window. Then the ball would be confiscated and the offender would get the strap - again!

EDUCATION ACT

The 1944 Education Act had reorganized all the schools in England and Wales. It said that all children had to go to primary school from the age of 5. At the age of 11, children took an exam called the 11 Plus, to decide what sort of further education they would have. If they passed the exam they could go on to a grammar school or technical school. If they failed they would be sent to a secondary modern. About 1 in 5 children went to a grammar school.

Norma

I loved reading and read whatever I could find in the library. I particularly liked the Enid Blyton books, Just William and What Katy Did. When I was 11, we all did the 11 Plus exam for the grammar school. Very few children passed. While I went on to Rochester Grammar School for Girls, most of my friends went to the local secondary modern school.

David

My secondary school was called a senior secondary. I did not enjoy it much and left at 15. Most of my friends left school at 15 to take up apprenticeships in the shipyards. The girls took office jobs. Only people who were going on to university stayed on for the last two years.

BOARDING SCHOOLS

Children of wealthier families or those whose fathers were in the armed forces were often sent to boarding school.

Elizabeth

When I was 13 I was sent to a boarding school in Burnham-on-Sea. This picture shows me on my first day at the school. I very much enjoyed my school. We spent a lot of time outside; playing hockey on the beach and going for walks and picnics. Once a term we had a fire drill. We had to climb out of the window and go down the fire escape, it was quite exciting. In those days girls were not encouraged to stay on at school for the sixth form and when I left I went to do a secretarial course in Switzerland.

TRAVELLING

MOTORBIKES

By 1954 all rationing had stopped and people had more money to spend on luxuries such as motor vehicles. Motorbikes were still popular, being cheaper to buy and run than cars.

CARS

Many people bought a car for the first time in the 50s. This meant they could now travel further from their homes. In 1959 the first stretch of the MI motorway was opened between London and Birmingham.

• In 1956 there were 3.75 million cars in Great Britain. In 1997, there were 27 million.

David

My dad was an agent for Wolseley. This was a very popular type of car in the 50s. We had a Wolseley 25. We only really used the car at weekends. On Saturdays we would go into town to do some shopping and on Sundays we would go out for a drive and maybe have tea.

SEE LONDON
on a London Transport Sightseeing Bus Tour

2 HOURS - 20 MILES - 3/6 (children half price) EVERY DAY AT 11, 12, 2
3, 4 AND 5 FROM VICTORIA (BUCKINGHAM PALACE ROAD)

BUSES

Buses and coaches were still popular ways of getting around, but many other forms of transport were beginning to disappear. Trams, which had run along rails down most city streets were being replaced by double-decker buses.

Elizabeth

We often used to go and visit my grandmother who lived near Brighton. She would take us into the town to visit the pier and eat ice creams on the beach. Our favourite treat was to ride on the top deck of an open-top bus.

TRAINS

The 1950s was also the end of the age of the steam train. Steam trains were gradually replaced by diesel or electric ones. More and more goods were being carried by lorries and vans on the roads rather than by trains, so the amount of railway track started to be reduced. Rail travel would never be quite the same again.

HOLIDAYS

More and more families took holidays in the 1950s. Most people took their holidays in Britain, usually driving their cars to stay at farm houses in the country, or boarding houses by the sea.

David

The first holiday I remember was 30 miles away at Ayr. We stayed at a hotel and the first thing we did was book a beach hut. We spent all day on the beach: playing football, making sand castles or paddling - it was usually too cold to swim. We returned to the hotel for high tea, and then went into the town to the fairground or to see a summer show. The highlight was eating knickerbocker glories in a cafe!

Air travel had always been much too expensive for most families, but the 1950s saw the beginning of the foreign holiday. Cheap holiday flights abroad to Spain and France began in 1952. A week's holiday in Paris cost £24.

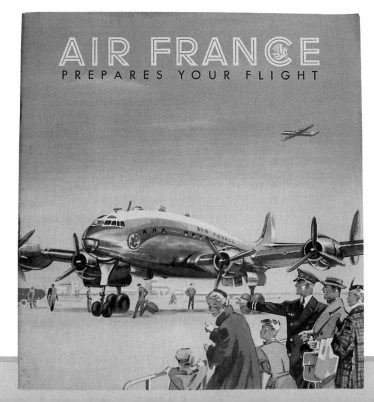

AIR FRANCE
PREPARES YOUR FLIGHT

By the end of the fifties, 2 million British people were spending their holidays abroad.

Allan

In 1958 my family went on a holiday to Europe. This was very unusual in those days and the whole neighbourhood turned out to wave us off. We travelled in our new car, an Austin A30. We drove down to London and crossed the Channel into France. We travelled through Austria, Switzerland, Germany, Belgium and Italy. It was very interesting because there was still a lot of evidence of the recent war.

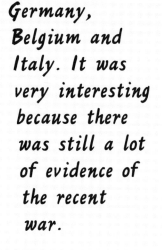

HAVING FUN

After the shortage of toys during the war, there was a larger quantity and variety in the 50s. Toys were very much divided into boys' and girls' toys. Boys played with model cars, train sets and Meccano sets. Girls played with dolls, some of whom had their own fashion wardrobe.

Allan

When I was five, my mum and dad gave me a tricycle for Christmas. I rode it everywhere.

My friend Ian and I were once given cowboy outfits. We spent many happy afternoons playing cowboys and Indians. We both pretended to be the Lone Ranger, a popular TV cowboy.

Elizabeth

My brother and sister and I loved playing in the garden and making up our own games. In the summer we would play tennis on the lawn or camp out in our tent, and in the winter there was often enough snow to go sledging.

COMICS

There was a wide choice of comics in the fifties. The *Dandy* and the *Beano* and *Enid Blyton's Magazine* were popular with younger children. The favourite amongst older boys was the *Eagle,* which covered a wide range of subjects, from westerns to war stories.

Norma

I used to get a comic called Tiny Tots. I once sent them some poems and was awarded the Tiny Tots Order of Merit by 'Uncle Jack'.

TELEVISION

At the beginning of the fifties, it was still quite unusual for people to have a television in their homes. But by the mid-fifties, television was replacing both the wireless and the cinema as a form of entertainment.

Norma

Television was not very important to me although I did enjoy watching 'I Love Lucy' on my aunt's TV next door. I also remember Muffin the Mule who was a string puppet.

The coronation of Queen Elizabeth II in June 1953, was one of the first historic ceremonies to be televised live.

It was watched all over the world, and even people who did not own television sets hired one to watch.

David

We were the only house in the street to have a television, so all our friends and neighbours came round to watch the coronation. The adults spent all day around the 'box', eating sandwiches and cakes. I was very bored. Every child at school was given a tin of toffees with a picture of the Queen on it.

CINEMA

In the early 50s the cinema was still very popular. Special Saturday morning programmes attracted children while teenagers went to see their favourite Hollywood movie stars.

THEN & NOW

• Early television screens were often only 20 cm (7 inches) wide. Today's widescreen TVs are about five times this width.

• In 1953, 16 per cent of households had a TV, now 99 per cent do.

• In the fifties there was only one TV channel, the BBC. Now there are five terrestrial channels, and hundreds of cable or satellite ones.

Most towns had cinemas and they often changed their programme two or three times a week. Many people used to go to the cinema three times a week! The most expensive tickets were 2/6 (12p) and the cheapest 1/6 (7p).

Danny Kaye in the film *Hans Christian Andersen*, 1952.

TEENAGERS

The word 'teenager' was not invented until the 1950s. Before then you were a child until you left school, got a job and became an adult. Suddenly there was a new group of people who had money to spend and a new way of life. The new teenagers had the freedom to rebel against their parents and choose their own music, film and fashion heroes.

MUSIC

It was America that was mainly responsible for the new style of music. Rock 'n' roll spread to Britain in 1955 with the song *Rock Around the Clock*. Teenagers danced in the aisles to Bill Haley and his Comets and the song stayed at Number 1 in the charts for many weeks.

David

We had a wind-up gramophone which my dad would get out on Sundays in winter. He would listen to old 40s records like Paul Robeson singing Ol' Man River. I preferred Bill Haley and his Comets.

Another huge musical phenomenon was Elvis Presley, who recorded his first single in 1954. He was idolised by teenagers throughout the world and joined the wave of other 50s stars such as Jerry Lee Lewis, Buddy Holly, Tommy Steele and Cliff Richard.

Norma

My mum loved popular music and we often had pop records playing in the kitchen. I was an Elvis Presley and Cliff Richard fan and saved up my pocket money to buy their records.

Coffee bars were popular places for teenagers to meet. They served new frothy Italian-style coffee and the lastest records could be listened to on the juke box. Youth clubs held dances every Saturday night with live bands playing and people dancing the quickstep or jive.

Teenagers have fun in a coffee bar in Soho.

FASHION

Children's fashions in the early fifties were not very exciting. Most clothes were made of uninteresting fabrics and were in dull colours.

Elizabeth

My sister and I usually wore dresses with cardigans on top. On our feet we wore sandals with white socks. Girls never wore trousers in those days. Young boys wore short trousers until they reached the age of about ten when they progressed to long ones.

After the drab war years when there was no money or material available, the 1950s saw a total change in fashion. For the first time there was a quite separate set of styles for young people.

Teenage girls started to wear full, bouncy skirts with petticoats underneath. These were perfect for dancing to rock 'n' roll. Many girls tried to hide their starched petticoats under their school uniforms! Shoes had thin stiletto heels, which often ruined floors and carpets.

Boys tried to look like their heroes, which led to many sporting Elvis Presley hair styles. Other young men copied the new 'Teddy Boy' image which consisted of tight trousers called 'drainpipes', narrow ties and long jackets, often trimmed with velvet.

Many boys copied the hairstyles of their pop heroes.

CLIFF SINGS No.1

mono

Cliff Sings

COLUMBIA
EXTENDED PLAY 45 r.p.m. RECORD

Clothing became much more fashionable and cheaper as chain stores such as Marks & Spencer and C & A spread across the country. Manufacturers realized that young people had money to spend and began to design clothes and write magazines for them.

IN THE NEWS

THE FESTIVAL OF BRITAIN

In 1951 a huge exhibition was held in London to show Britain's progress since the war. The Festival of Britain was designed to show what Britain had achieved in science, technology and design. It was intended to cheer the country up after the difficult years of the forties and to look to the future. There was a gigantic funfair, exhibitions of art and science and a number of strange buildings like the Dome of Discovery. The Royal Festival Hall is a building that remains from that time.

FESTIVAL OF BRITAIN

1951
MAY 3 - SEPTEMBER 30

- Over 8 million people visited the festival during the five months it was open. 6 million people visited the Millennium Dome in 2000.

- It cost 5 shillings (25p) to visit the Festival. It cost £20 to visit the Millennium Dome.

CONQUERING EVEREST

On 1 June 1953, Edmund Hillary and sherpa Tenzing Norgay became the first men to reach the summit of Mount Everest. The mountain, the highest on Earth is 8,848 metres high (29,029 feet). The news reached Queen Elizabeth on the eve of her coronation day, 2 June.

Edmund Hillary and Tenzing enjoy a snack on their return down the mountain.

Elizabeth

We had no television in our house, but we went round to a neighbour to watch the news of Edmund Hillary's Everest ascent and see the coronation of the Queen. It was a very exciting couple of days.

THE SPACE RACE

The first ever artificial satellite was launched into space on 4 October 1957 by Russia. This was part of the great space race in which many countries were competing to get the first craft into space. The satellite, called *Sputnik 1*, travelled at 28,800 km per hour (18,000 mph), and could circle the Earth in 1 hour 35 minutes.

LOOKING TO THE FUTURE

After the war years of the forties, the fifties were a great improvement for most people. Unemployment was low, nearly all men had jobs and families were far better off. New machines made housework easier for women. The shops were full of exciting new clothes, foods and machines, and people had the money to buy them.

► Holidaymakers enjoy summer on the beach at Blackpool.

The opening of the first motorway in 1959 paved the way for transport of the future.

For most people the fifties was a time of plenty with many new inventions and time to enjoy them.

• Unemployment in the fifties was never more than 400,000. Unemployment in 2000 was around 1 million.

Further Reading

Take Ten Years - 1950s; Margaret Sharman, Evans Brothers

Fifty Years Ago series - *At Home, Having Fun, Going on a Trip, In the High Street*; Hodder Wayland

20th Century Fashion -40s and 50s; Cally Blackman, Heinemann 1999

A Family in the Fifties; Andrew Langley, Hodder Wayland 1986

The Fifties; Tom Stacy, Hodder Wayland 1989

Fiction:

Amber's Secret; Ann Pilling, Collins 2000

After the War was Over; Michael Foreman, Pavilion 1995

Glossary

apprenticeship: Being taken on as a junior in a company to learn a trade.

chain stores: A series of shops owned by the same company and selling the same type of goods.

council estates: Areas of housing owned by the council and rented out to people.

decimalization: The introduction of a new system of money in 1971.

Eleven Plus: An exam children sat aged 11 to decide which school they would go on to.

gramophone: A machine that played records.

juke box: A machine that plays a record when money is inserted.

rationing: The sharing out of food and other goods during the war.

slum housing: Very poor or run-down housing.

Teddy Boys: Young men who dressed in Edwardian-style clothes.

unemployed: Without a job.

INDEX